A to Z of

121 UNCONVENTIONAL MANAGEMENT CONCEPTS

A to Z of

121 UNCONVENTIONAL MANAGEMENT CONCEPTS

Rakhshanda Jalil

NIYOGI
BOOKS

Published by:

NIYOGI BOOKS
D-78, Okhla Industrial Area, Phase-I
New Delhi 110 020, India
Tel.: 91-11-26816301, 49327000
Fax: 91-11-26810483, 91-11-26813830
e-mail: niyogibooks@gmail.com
www.niyogibooks.com

Design: Write Media

ISBN: 978-81-89738-03-7
Year of Publication: 2006
Second Impression: 2012

Printed at: Niyogi Offset Pvt. Ltd., New Delhi, India

Contents

Preface

There is no magic formula for management. Management is at best an inexact science dependent upon several variables, and managers are some of the most misunderstood of all God's creatures. There is no such thing as a perfect manager. No one has a patent on a hundred per cent error-proof system of management. If they claim to have one, they are lying.

The only time-tested formula you can bring to your personal management equation is – Experience. Perhaps, one day you too can compile your own handbook of management – an A-Z based on your own uniquely personal experiences – to hand over to those who follow in your footsteps. Meanwhile, go through this selection with an open mind.

When you read this book you will agree that it deals with the 'constants' of business: those ingredients that never change or date. This is not one of those books that you read once and put on the shelf. It is the sort you can dip into – again and again. The more you thumb through it, the more you will benefit from it; you will see newer patterns emerge, new perspectives on old issues that will startle you afresh with their simplicity and fresh insights from some of the greatest minds down the ages.

There is something for everyone here. It doesn't matter if you are the president of a multinational company, or a small-time exporter of spare parts or a young and struggling entrepreneur trying to find your feet in a market swamped with inexpensive dumped foreign goods. You can pick and choose whatever you find useful from this storehouse of unconventional wisdom, combine it with what you already have stored in your experience bank and come up with the winning combination: your own custom-made management tool that works best for you. Let this book be the beginning of a journey.

Wishing you every success as you travel towards your goal,

Rakhshanda Jalil
Jamia Millia Islamia
New Delhi, 2006

A

ability

There is only one proof of ability – results. Men with ability in action almost always achieve results. Your ability is nothing more than your God-given talents and potential that you have chosen to develop.

Remember, all abilities are like plants that need pruning by study and diligence. Even so-called natural abilities need a gentle push in the right direction to bear fruit.

What sets apart the champions from the survivors, the successful from the mediocre, the man at the top from those languishing at the middle orders, is the direct ability to show what they are by what they do with what they have. Ability, then, is rated by what a person finishes or accomplishes rather than what he attempts.

advertising

Someone rightly said, 'When business is good it pays to advertise; when it is bad you have got to advertise.' The advertising industry is one of our most basic forms of communication and information. It is a different matter that much of this information is purveyed not to inform but to manipulate and to achieve a single objective – to make somebody think that he needs something that very possibly he doesn't have, or make someone think one version of something is better than another when it may or may not actually be so. Yet no one disputes the fact that advertising is vital to business. In fact, doing business without advertising is a bit like winking at a girl in the dark. You know what you are doing, but she doesn't. Business today is not about persuading one or two or three customers but getting in the crowds:

He who has a thing to sell
And goes and whispers in a well,
Is not apt to get the dollars
As he who climbs a tree and hollers.

ambition

Thomas Alva Edison had said, 'Show me a thoroughly satisfied man and I will show you a failure.' A man without ambition is dead. When a man is no longer anxious to do better than well, he is done for. In the corporate context more so, for unless you are willing to drench yourself completely in your work far beyond the capacity of an average man, you are just not cut out for a position at the top. Don't be afraid to take a big step if you are convinced it is required; you can't cross a chasm in two small steps. Make no little plans. They have no magic; they can't stir your blood and rouse you to great heights. Make big plans; aim high. Remember, all ambitions are lawful barring those built on the miseries of others. The plain fact is that human beings are happy only when they are striving for something worthwhile, the operating word being 'worthwhile'.

analogies

More than half of the 'Fortune 500' companies, including household names such as Procter & Gamble, IBM, Shell and Singer, periodically undertake some kind of creative experiments and R&D. They review some of history's most notable discoveries to determine if a pattern of discovery can be determined. In many cases, the intuitive spark can be traced to an analogy. For instance, Newton saw the apple fall to the ground and established the force of gravity; Einstein struck upon his Theory of Relativity while riding a train and absently watching another train pull ahead at a faster speed, giving him the sense of moving backwards – relatively that is. Analogies stir new ideas and concepts using concrete images rather than abstraction. Analogies can be the catalysts for new growth or modifications in your organisation or industry too. All you have to do is to look around for inspiration.

Our ancient texts, the Ramayana, Mahabharata, the Vedas and Shastras are a veritable storehouse of analogies that can be put to creative use in today's corporate world. Expressions such as Lakshman Rekha, Chakravyuh, etc., have passed into common usage even in the business world.

appraisal

Staff appraisals are gaining increasing importance as a contributor to the success of organisations worldwide. Increased competition, rapid changes, reduced resources and employee expectations have all combined in such a way that organisations are being expected to achieve more with less. Periodic appraisals are an ideal mechanism to first gauge people's commitment towards achieving the stated aims of the organisation, and then gain their confidence and commitment. The objective of the appraisal is to help improve individual performance, realise potential and achieve better results for the organisation.

auto-suggestion

Any thought that is passed on to the subconscious often enough and convincingly enough is finally accepted. It becomes the dominant thought in one's mind. This is known as auto-suggestion. You can decide what will be your ruling mantra in life. You can tell yourself over and over again: 'I can do it,' 'I can win,' 'I will be happy no matter what'. Make your own list of constructive and positive statements. Use them regularly, repeatedly, consistently and constructively. Remember, no flame of desire can continue to burn vigorously if its supply of suggestive fuel is cut off from it. Similarly, you may want to do something, but if you don't tell yourself repeatedly and constructively to do it, it will never get done. You can't always control your thoughts, but you can certainly control your words. Repeating certain words over and over again impresses them on your subconscious and you are then master of the situation.

B

behaviour

Sometimes you can't help the way you feel, but you can certainly help the way you think and act, in short the way you behave (see Auto-Suggestion). If you change your behaviour, it will in turn, change the way you feel. Here's what you can do for starters:

- Be understanding – don't expect to be understood.
- Be interested – don't try to be interesting.
- Be pleasing – don't expect to be pleased.
- Be entertaining – don't expect to be loved.
- Be helpful – don't expect to be helped.

blame

Finding a scapegoat when things begin to go wrong is the easiest thing to do. Yet apportioning blame or finding the right candidate to shoulder the guilt is not the most constructive thing to do. Pointing the finger at an individual or laying the burden of blame at anyone's door in a public declaration can be counter-productive. The need to lay blame is often the symptom rather than the laying of the blame. When within a group it becomes necessary to blame someone, the process of disintegration has already set in. By laying blame, other members of the group hope to absolve themselves by using words such as 'he/she' or 'they' instead of 'I' or 'we'. This further gives rise to schisms and cliques, and eventually 'politicking'. An effective manager has to steer a middle path between blame and irresponsibility. The right word for this middle path can be accountability. If each individual is accountable for his or her actions, there will be no need for witch-hunting.

burnout

Too much money. Too much work. Too much success, too soon. Repetition, boredom and fatigue. These are the banes of corporate high fliers. Lack of motivation, loss of appetite, listlessness, heart attack and other stress-related diseases – these are the classic symptoms of burnout. You can only go so far. Where do you go from the top? You expend so much energy in reaching the top, and you are in such a tearing hurry to beat everybody else to get there, that when you make it up there, there is precious little left inside you to enjoy the feeling of being on top. You can try buying diamond necklaces for your wife or send your children to expensive vacations abroad or buy a Rolex or BMW for yourself – but nothing really matters, not deep inside. That is when, if you want to continue being a flesh-and-blood person and not a robot, you have to do something to deal with your burnout. Take a long hard look at yourself, your life and priorities, introduce small, vital changes in your routine, go away for a restful holiday, start going for walks – in fact, try anything that will re-charge your batteries and bring the zest back into your life.

business

The art of winning in business lies in working hard. Anybody can cut prices, but it takes much more to be a cut above the rest. In the world of business, success is important, profitability vital, strategy is king and accuracy means everything. To be a success in business, be daring, be first, be different. Have a competitive advantage over all others. Winston Churchill had said, 'Some people regard private enterprise as a predatory tiger to be shot. Others look on it as a cow to milk. Not enough people see it as a healthy horse, pulling a sturdy wagon.' At the same time, business without profit is not a business any more than a pickle is a candy! As the famous Greek shipping tycoon, Aristotle Onassis, had said, 'The secret of business is to know something that nobody else knows.'

C

can't-do myths

Some of the most popular Can't-Do myths in today's world of business are: 'That's much too radical.'; 'Why stick your neck out.'; 'We tried it once and it didn't work.'; 'We need to follow the rules.'; 'That is contrary to policy.'; 'Do you have any statistics to back that up.'; etc, etc. Can't-Do myths are used most often by people who lack initiative and drive. The 'Can-Do' types, on the other hand, look at business a little differently. They always ask themselves how they can find ways to outsmart the competitors and give themselves the competitive edge.

cause and effect

This fundamental law controls everything in the universe. For every cause there is an effect and there are consequences for everything we think, say or do, or don't do or neglect to do. According to this law, there are no accidents. We are totally responsible for our lives; nothing happens 'just like that'. The seeming accidents, the so-called freak and inexplicable events are simply things for which we don't have enough information to give a logical explanation. People, unfortunately, want to take credit for the positive outcomes of their decisions and tend to find a scapegoat or someone to blame for things that go wrong. But the Law of Cause and Effect states that we are totally responsible for our lives, answerable for our actions and accountable for our decisions (see responsibility).

change

No skill is more vital to a manager than the ability to successfully implement change since for most people change is synonymous with threat and instability. Status quo is much more comfortable for those who have rigid habits and convenient ways of doing things. It is often necessary to create a threat to motivate people to change. At the same time, managers must be equally mindful not to create too much of a threat that they paralyse those whose support is needed or to disrupt the balance of power so much that the strengths offered by the status quo are eroded. Remember to give details of the coming change and explain the reasons for it. Let employees ask questions, express opinions and concerns.

commitment

Instilling pride in what they do and the organisation

they work for is a big step towards winning employees' enthusiastic commitment to their jobs. Explaining your organisation's vision and strategy also helps. The more they know about the progress of your company the more they can contribute. When people are kept informed, they begin to think, and that is when they come up with new ideas. Take quality, for instance. The well-trained employee who understands the larger picture of the company and of the product itself will build better quality into it. If employees know what they are supposed to be looking out for, they and the organisation would be far better off in the long run. Through a simple matter of attitude and communication, an effective manager can instill commitment in the employees, and a sense of belonging to the organisation that employs them.

competition

Take a long hard look at your competitors. Competition can be a positive thing and need not be seen as the devil incarnate snapping at your heels. For one thing, it encourages you to put in your best by pushing you to your utmost limits. By acting as a motivating force, it often forces you to change with the times. Best of all, competition gives you a yardstick to measure yourself against. Remember the golden rule of business: If you know your product or service well and are also abreast of what the competition is doing, then the ball is in your court. You are sure to come out a winner if you play your shots right.

complainers

Most organisations have their share of chronic complainers. Nothing makes them happy except more things to complain about. They whine about everything – about their job, about the work they are required to do, about the people they are expected to work with, even about the air-conditioning that is too high or too low for their liking! People like this can wear you down. You can fire them only if their work is exceptionally poor. However, usually, the average complainer does little to justify outright dismissal. First of all, don't take complainers personally. It isn't you they have a grudge against; it is the whole wide world. If their complaining is hurting morale or production, then it is time for you to act. Talk straight with them. Let them know in no uncertain terms that it is this far and no further. Tell them flatly their unnecessary complaining will not be tolerated, and then follow it up.

concentration

Concentration, or calming the mind makes movements automatic. This is important in most sports. The most accomplished players claim their peak performances never occur when they are consciously thinking of how to perform. Inspired games, they say, are played with unthinking spontaneity, so that years of experience and training are compressed into split seconds of decision-making. The same is true of seasoned businessmen. At vital moments involving crores of rupees, it is often calming the mind through concentration that helps in making the right decision. Focusing on the future may provide direction and enthusiasm in any venture, but there is nothing like concentrating on the present to improve performance.

confluence

At some time or other we have all experienced what we call the 'magic moment' – when everything seems to fall into place, when several good things seem to be happening to us all at once. Such magic moments also represent what is known as confluence, or the coming together of a number of conditions and events. Scientists have called these moments by different names such as synchronicity, seriality, clustering or coincidence. Anyway, accept the idea that good things happen in bunches. Learn to recognise these good things and to stretch your luck when they are happening. Conversely, learn to be cautious when bad things are happening. Carefully weigh actions and decisions so that good developments pile up and bad ones are not allowed to cluster.

controlled aggression

The right use of power can be defined as controlled aggression. Consider the contrast: uncontrolled power is a destructive force, but power that is finely tuned can be used for creative purposes. For this, power has to be first communicated positively, not as an extension of brute force or as a series of threats. Increasingly, management specialists have come to agree that the last method to be used on the donkey is to beat him with a stick. Ideas and motivation must come across with the least amount of tension and hostility possible. That is when controlled aggression becomes important. Only the masterly leader can turn this kind of power that is so potentially destructive into a creative and positive force. Aggressiveness is a necessary quality of executive life. Without it there would be no initiative, no competitiveness, and no progress. But it has to be cloaked in tact, kindness and empathy – the proverbial iron hand in the velvet glove.

courage

Courage is a special kind of knowledge – the knowledge of how to fear what ought to be feared and how not to fear what ought not to be feared. Nothing worthwhile in this world is ever achieved without courage. True greatness, be it in winning boardroom battles, building a family business or leaving a legacy of trust, is largely braveness. It requires courage to escape from old ideas and old standards and respectable time-honoured ways of doing things. You gain courage, strength and confidence by every experience in which you really stop to look fear in the face.

You are able to say to yourself, 'I have lived through this. I can take the next thing that comes along.' Courage is not the absence of fear, but the conquest of it.

counselling

Most organisations have some form of performance

appraisal for their employees. However, very few, at least in India, offer any form of counselling. Most managers keep end-of-the-year assessments a carefully guarded secret and do very little about it. Others fret and fume about the inadequacies in the performance of their subordinates. The majority of managers rarely communicate their appraisal to subordinates. As a result, performance appraisals become a one-way street ending in a blind alley. The way out of this no-win situation is counselling. It affords an opportunity to search for unrealised abilities. It helps the manager to know his subordinates better. Periodic counselling gives excellent opportunities for a manager to talk with his employees to enhance the chances of achieving mutual goals and of generating among subordinates a greater desire to take responsibility for their own growth and performance. In a performance review the emphasis is on the objective facts of effective job behaviour. Counselling, on the other hand, is concerned with the attitudes and feelings about such facts and behaviour. Long neglected in India, counselling is essential for an individual's growth; and the growth of society and industry rests primarily on individual growth.

creativity

Most of us tend to cling to the old and resist the new. Fear, ignorance and indolence become barriers to growth – within ourselves and our organisations. Most of us think of creativity as a brilliant breakthrough, as a radical departure from tradition, as the original idea that stands out sharply from the daily grind of routine by its sheer novelty. It need not necessarily be so. Creativity means having the latitude to exercise imagination, ingenuity and initiative. Such creative thinking is encouraged or discouraged by the atmosphere that is set by the man at the top.

crisis management

Organisations, like people, go through crises. How well they weather a crisis has a lot to do with the ways in which power and authority are used for what is called crisis management. Most people avoid a crisis as though it were a plague. But for someone aiming for leadership, crisis is a golden opportunity to prove your worth, to step into the breach and become the hero of the hour. Remember these lines from Rudyard Kipling's poem called *"If":*

If you can keep your head when all about you
Are losing theirs and blaming it on you,
If you can trust yourself when all men doubt you
But make allowances for their doubting too;
If you can wait and not be tired by waiting,
Yours is the Earth and everything that is in it,
And – which is more – you will be a Man, my son!

Crisis management will give you just the right opportunity to prove your mettle and, what is more, forge a break from the normal routine. So welcome the opportunity; it may be heaven-sent.

D

decisiveness

How important to a manager is the ability to make decisions? Lee Iococco, the legendary chairman of Chrysler, put it best when he said, 'If I had to sum up in one word what makes a good manager, I'd say decisiveness. You can use the fanciest computers to gather the numbers, but in the end you have to set a timetable and act. And I don't mean rashly. I am sometimes described as a flamboyant leader and a hip-shooter, a fly-by-the-seat-of-pants operator. But if that were true, I could never have been successful in this business.'

delegation

You can't possibly do everything yourself – no matter how important your job may be or how efficient you might think you are. You have to delegate some part of your workload and the responsibilities that go with it – to whom and at what stage, of course, remains at your own discretion. Delegation is not the same as 'giving out work'. You delegate when you deliberately choose to give your staff the authority to carry out some part of your work that you could have decided to keep with yourself.

With delegation goes a necessary part of authority, responsibility and also accountability. Successful delegation means matching responsibility with authority. The person to whom the work has been delegated has to take a certain amount of accountability too with the job, but the overall responsibility remains with the manager. The buck always stops with him, not with the delegatee!

determination

Hannibal the Great had said, 'We will either find a way, or make one.' Nothing is impossible if you have the desire and the determination to achieve something. Nothing in the world can take the place of persistence.

So press on. Talent alone will not take you very far; nothing in the world is more common than unsuccessful men with talent. Neither will genius; unrewarded genius is a proverb. Education, too, is not of much use on its own; the world is full of educated people.

Persistence and determination are what truly matter in the long run.

discipline

Discipline can be enforced only by someone who wields authority correctly, otherwise it is very easy to misuse it. First of all, be consistent with your discipline. If you let one person get away and throw the rulebook at another for breaking the same rule, you are going to create a morale problem among your staff. Make the penalty fit the crime. If it is a serious offence, you have to come down really hard. But don't be too harsh for what amounts to a trivial offence. Some managers paint themselves into a corner with a series of written rules that don't leave any margin for decision-making. Allow for exceptions. Maybe there is a legitimate reason for a particular wrongdoing. Find out. It is human to get angry, but it may not always be in your best interests to lose your temper. A good manager must know how to control his temper and when to pick the right moment for expressing it.

drive

Drive is a universal attribute of all successful men. It is made up of many things: an urge to make things happen; high standards of performance and expectation; dissatisfaction with the conventional; a restless search for a better way to get things done. Drive is more than a response to external stimuli; it is self-motivated and comes from deep within the person. The man with drive is not compelled by a succession of incentives such as a promotion or a company lease or a new car. He has a kind of compulsiveness, a tenacious persistence to follow through and get the job done – at all costs! Compare him with the man of promise who fails at the crucial moment; that man fails not because he does not want to perform, but because he assumes his superior intelligence will get the job done. He sits back because he lacks the drive to expend the extra effort. Drive, then, is a matter of going that little bit further and pushing ahead that crucial half inch when it really matters. Men with drive make things happen when their fellow-workers are content to let things happen to them.

E

employees

Always remember one golden rule about employees: how you select people is always more important than how you manage them once they are on the job. If you start with the right people, you will have fewer problems with them than later on. If you hire the wrong people (never mind if they are MBAs or engineers from reputed institutions) you are going to be in trouble sooner or later and all the revolutionary techniques they may have learnt at fancy management schools will not bail you out. The right degree is not necessarily the right qualification for the right job.

encouragement

The finest gift you can give someone is encouragement.

Not everyone gets the encouragement they need to reach their full potential. A word of encouragement is like oxygen to the soul. Good work can never be expected out of people without periodic encouragement.

Note how good you feel when you have encouraged someone else. No other argument is then necessary to suggest that you should never miss the opportunity to give encouragement when it is due. Correcting someone when they are wrong achieves much, but encouraging them when they do right achieves far more.

enthusiasm

Enthusiasm is the electric current that keeps the engine of life going at top speed. It is the propeller of all success. Enthusiasm is that kindling spark that marks the difference between the leaders in every activity and the laggards who put in just enough effort to 'get by'. Yet no one can keep their enthusiasm going at top gear automatically. It must continually be nourished with new actions, new aspirations, new efforts, new vision. If you had enthusiasm for your work once, but now you don't, maybe it is your own fault; you neglected to feed it.

When your enthusiasm lights
Your ambition's fire
People will come from miles around
To watch you burn.

environment

The environment in which you work can sometimes

make or break you. At the same time, a successful man is one who rises above the confines of his environment to reach his full potential. The first step towards real success is when you refuse to be captive of the environment in which you find yourself. Often, people blame their environment for their failures and setbacks whereas they have only themselves to blame. Reasonable people adapt themselves to the environment around them; unreasonable people either persist in trying to make the environment adapt to them or in fighting against the environment that they consider unsuitable. To a large extent, we are all products of our environment. We cannot choose our home environment, but we can certainly choose our work environment. So, choose the environment that will best develop you towards your objective. Are the things around you helping you towards success, or are they holding you back?

experience

Who is in a better position to analyse the competition, come up with winning ideas, and train new employees than the person who has been around for a long time? New-age western corporations need to learn a thing or two from Asian economies where valuing older people is part of our *samskara*. There is a wealth of experience that comes with age. People don't become obsolete; equipments and methods do. It is a lot more expensive to train and develop a younger worker than it is to give the job to an older, experienced employee. There is also a big difference in the work ethic of an older and more experienced person and a younger employee. Experience tells you that success does not come overnight; you have to slog long and hard for it. Creating temporary or part-time jobs can be mutually beneficial for the employees and the organisation. Don't make the mistake of treating this as charity; you are tapping a mine of experience. For age and obsolescence don't go together, though experience and wisdom usually do.

F

failure

Fear of failure can be corrosive. It can block insight and keep self-confidence from being converted into positive action. As someone once said, 'Winning means being unafraid to lose.' Coming to realise this can be a liberating experience because it allows you to take chances, follow your hunches and allow new ideas to blossom. Failure can be converted into something positive, it can be treated as a new learning experience. You can learn a lot from losing – provided you take the right approach. Guilt, denial or depression has to be avoided at all costs.

fear

The fear of criticism, the fear of ridicule, the fear of losing face in front of colleagues and subordinates, and worst of all, the fear of failure can be a recurring nightmare for many. When people feel threatened and anxious, they become even more rigid in their outlook, and when in doubt they become more dogmatic. They find it easier to either retreat into a shell or simply dig their heels in and become stubborn instead of facing their fears. Some people spend most of their working lives in fear of making a mistake. This makes them so timid, so closed to new ideas that they are afraid of being creative or original. Others are fearful of anything that is complicated, or seems complicated. They would much rather go for the simple and straightforward than attempt to wrestle with the new and seemingly difficult.

The only way to fight your fear is to confront it and understand it. Do what you fear and your fear will disappear. If you are scared of using the state-of-the-art computer, stay back after office hours and come to grips with it. Or get someone to explain how it works. The longer you put off confronting your fear, the more frightening it will become – inside your head!

flexibility

Flexibility should not be confused with inconsistency. It actually involves a productive sort of contrariness: the ability to be cautiously bold by eliminating all unnecessary hazards while still taking chances: also to be ambiguously clear by defining a goal while allowing plenty of manoeuvring space for reaching the goal. You can be flexible and still retain the right to make the final decision. Sometimes it is wise to steer clear of setting down policies or rules that are so hard and fast as to be unworkable. If someone breaks a rule that seems unfair, consider changing it. A manager has to be more flexible and open-minded when the going is not so good. Some managers take the opposite approach and end up either with a disintegrated empire or a bunch of robots who are afraid to take a decision. These are the times when flexibility has to be the name of the game and when managers should be looking for more inputs from employees, not less.

G

genius

Genius lies in the ability to reduce the complicated to the simple. To do easily what is difficult for others is the mark of talent. To do what is impossible for talent is the mark of genius. Genius does what it must, while talent does what it can. Genius does not create – it discovers. It can reduce the complicated to the simple, the hidden to the obvious and the impossible to the possible. The principal mark of genius is not perfection but originality, the opening of new frontiers.

goals

The starting point in building an effective organisation is to be found in three basic questions: Why is the company in business? What are its objectives? What is the company attempting to accomplish? Answers to these questions define the common task and provide the framework into which each jobholder's work will fit like a giant jigsaw puzzle. Goal-setting and role-setting, therefore, go hand in hand. So should corporate and individual goals (see Teamwork). Here are some self-confronting questions you can ask yourself to better evaluate your goals:

- Where do I want to be at any given time?
- How am I going to get there?
- What do I have to do to get myself from where I am to where I want to be?
- What is the first small step I can take to get going?

good timing

The gift of good timing depends on more than hearing opportunity knock. It means being able to catch the sound of the first faint tap – and act upon it. Ill-timed, either premature or tardy, even the most brilliant or creative ideas can fall flat. Inbuilt protective instincts (see Intuition) can also help in knowing precisely when to act.

In today's fickle world, if necessity is the mother of invention, economic volatility is its father.

Nowhere is it more apparent than in developing economies. That puts even more premium on intuitive timing, on accurately reading the various economic signals and pouncing on the right one. The reverse also applies – for good timing lies in knowing when to pounce and when to hold back.

goodwill

We will confine ourselves here to the definition of goodwill in the legal sense for even a novice in any profession would know of the immense benefits of a good name generated through mere word of mouth. Goodwill has been defined as 'the benefit arising from connection or reputation' of an existing business.

While it clearly has a monetary value, it is not always easy to quantify. Lawyers have distinguished between 'cat goodwill' and 'dog goodwill'. The former is goodwill attached to premises that occupy a convenient or valuable site for particular business purposes, while the latter is goodwill that is based on the special knowledge or skill of the people running a business. 'Cat goodwill' can only be sold with the business, while 'dog goodwill' is either not saleable at all, or if saleable, implies that some human know-how or other information is being sold with the tangible assets of a business.

gossip

Office gossip can range from the harmless, lunchtime chatter to something far more malicious. The thing to remember is that he who gossips to you will gossip about you. Gossip is the torpedo that has sunk many budding careers. As someone rightly said:

Gossip is a deadly microbe
It has neither legs nor wings
It is composed mostly of tales
And most of them have stings!

In a work context, it is wiser to say little by way of idle talk – for if you talk about yourself you are a bore, and if you talk about others you are a gossip!

growth

Growth means change and change involves risks, stepping from the known to the unknown. Strength and growth come only through continuous effort and struggle. Just as fire is the test of gold, adversity is the test of strong men. It is the difficulties, the rough patches, the unexpected obstacles and the unforeseen crises that show men what they are and shape their growth. All growth, then, depends upon activity. There is no development without effort, just as there is no growth without struggle.

H

habits

Someone has rightly said that the easier it is to do, the harder it is to change. The right habits, if wisely and skillfully formed, become truly a second nature. Similarly, the wrong habits can become the bane of a lifetime. In the work context too, the right habits of discipline, punctuality, organisation, methodicalness, etc., can stand you in good stead. Sometimes it is easier and quicker to do something the way you have always been doing it out of sheer habit. You may know that it is not the best way to do things, but it takes time and effort to break old habits. Habits are not something you can toss out of the window one fine morning; they have to be coaxed gently and firmly to go away, one step at a time. Get into the habit of being strict with yourself; demand a certain standard of performance; approve of yourself, even reward yourself if you meet your standards. We are what we repeatedly do. Excellence is not an art; it can become a habit.

hands-on approach

Go beyond listening and finding out what the trouble is to advising and acting immediately. A true hands-on attitude is when you learn to do something on the job – whether it is work-related like removing a bottleneck or personal, like doing something to help an employee with a drinking problem. These are just two random examples. As a manager you are faced with a mind-boggling variety of problems and it is your job to find suitable solutions.

human behaviour

Like the weather, and like human beings themselves, human behaviour is highly variable. Yet mankind has found it useful, in fact necessary, to predict both the weather and human behaviour. As a manager your most basic tool is your ability to first of all understand the men and women who work with you or for you. For that you have to know their feelings, attitudes and, yes, also their emotions. In today's fast-changing work ethos, business executives all over the world are drawing on psychology and other behavioural sciences to find solutions to perplexing human problems. The motto of one of the most successful Japanese companies is: 'People are our most important asset.' With India carving a place for itself in the global market, there is growing consciousness to draw the utmost from each worker in a way that is mutually beneficial. Management books abound with new theories stressing motivation, group dynamics and a host of other human processes. We sometimes tend to forget that many of these so-called 'new concepts' were outlined by our forefathers in our ancient texts. Two thousand years ago, the Indian statesman, Kautilya, wrote a treatise called *Arthshastra*, where the basis of all governance, he said, is 'knowing people' (see Insight).

hunch

Hunch is a vague, unprofessional sort of word to the professional manager. It seems to imply betting on horses or speculating on the stock market. Yet, even in today's empirical world of business where systems' analysts and computers can compute the risk-reward ratios of any decision, the old-fashioned hunch continues to be an important though often unappreciated managerial tool. Logic, training and analysis can lead you only partly down the path to a profitable decision. The last step to success frequently requires a daring, intuitive leap, as many chief executives who control the destinies of the world's biggest organisations will reluctantly concede. Sometimes, it requires guts to follow a good hunch, to be able to say, 'I don't know, but I can feel it.' But since management is an inexact science, frequently defined as the art of making decisions with insufficient information, even the most cautious boss is sometimes forced to act on nebulous, inner impressions. That is what a hunch is all about.

I

insight

It means the ability to see 'into' situations or people. Insight in this sense is synonymous with understanding and discernment. It is an ability fused with intelligence, though it is by no means a marker for intelligence-related tests. Bright people frequently have blurred understanding or insight into others. Some mediocre people, on the other hand, often have sharp or intuitive discernment. Insightful managers learn to combine their God-given inborn qualities with the fruits of experience to create effective management tools. Thoughtful hindsight of past experiences and careful analysis of current problems and opportunities can be far more fruitful, if managers can bring to bear all the insight they are capable of. The end result can be effective foresight.

intuition

The athlete speaks of mind and movement coalescing. The Zen Buddhist describes the sound of one hand clapping. The successful businessman talks about his gut feeling. Their vocabularies differ but they are all talking of the same hazy, indistinct, subliminal impression that enables one individual to peer up into the night sky and see a faint twinkling star while equally intelligent colleagues see only the blackness. So what is this mystical power, this magical faculty, this guardian angel that is smarter than us and can take care of us, provided it is allowed to function? Intuition can be simply described as knowledge gained without rational thought.

The late business philosopher, R. Buckminster Fuller, called it 'cosmic fishing'. But he warned, 'Once you feel a nibble, you've got to hook the fish. Too many people,' he said, 'get a hunch, then light up a cigarette and forget about it.' Don't ignore your inner voice; respect it enough to give it a patient hearing. If you understand, nurture and above all trust your intuition, you can turn it into your most powerful business tool.

isolation

Isolation at the top is a well-known phenomenon and a major hazard facing chief executives. Subordinates hesitate to knock on the CEO's door, especially if they are the bearer of bad news. Smart executives learn to keep an ear cocked for what the grapevine is saying and are quick at listening to the rumblings from below. Like warning bells going off inside you, these rumblings – faint at first – are often portents of large-scale disasters. Isolation at the top can not only cause deafness to these voices of discontent, it can often breed a dangerous illusion of immunity among those less careful – a 'this-can't-happen-to-me' syndrome. Remember, not only is it very lonely at the top, there is no rung on the way up the ladder that prepares you for the downward tumble.

J

job description

Do you know what your job involves? Does your manager know what you are doing? And you, as a manager, do you know that your staff know what they should be doing? It can be that as a job-holder or as a manager you are not completely aware of the demands and content of your job. A written job description can be of enormous help – both to the employee and the employer. Not only does it help to give focus to the tasks at hand, it is a useful aid when it comes to delegation, appraisal and maintenance. It can also include the extent of authority to take decisions and show initiative. From the manager's point of view, a job description can highlight 'gaps' or 'overlaps' in tasks, present an opportunity for re-designing or re-organising work practices, identify training needs and provide a focus for target setting.

K

kaleidoscopic vision

A good manager needs 'kaleidoscopic vision' or the ability to see new patterns in old phenomena. He can take a set of existing fragments, twist them, shake them around and come up with an exciting new view. This inward-viewing process is similar to the Zen Buddhist way of looking at things: peering into the essential nature of a phenomenon until an illuminating new perception (satori) suddenly smites the conscious mind.

knowledge

Know your product. Make it your business to know every single detail about your product or service before you step into the big bad world of big business. People say: 'Know yourself'; sometimes it is better to 'Know others too.' That is the one cardinal rule of business. Someone once said, 'Knowledge is power', but mere knowledge is not power; it is only possibility. Action is power and its highest manifestation is when it is directed by knowledge. Like religion, knowledge must be 'experienced' in order to be known really and truly.

L

lateral thinking

Edward de Bono, the guru of lateral thinking, has said, 'Thinking is a skill; it can be developed and improved if one knows how.' In a best-selling book he has described lateral thinking as creative thinking or allowing the mind to generate as many alternative approaches as it can.

Vertical thinking is sequential (a→b→c); lateral thinking can make jumps (a→c).

The good thing about lateral thinking is that one does not have to be correct at every step.

With vertical thinking one concentrates on a single point and excludes what is irrelevant; with lateral thinking one welcomes chance intrusions.

leadership

Do you want to be a leader or a follower? No one is born a leader. People who have become successful executives have learnt the art of leading and inspiring others. They are people who are not content to belong to the mob of followers, but rather want to be part of that precious commodity that the world hungers for today – that of executive leadership. Napoleon's famous remark, 'Every soldier in my army carries a Marshal's baton in his knapsack…' was never truer than it is today. Everyone has the potential of leadership and executive ability inside them. What is needed is to bring these qualities out. The formula for success in leadership is: Plan to win. Your watchwords should be: power, luck, ability, nonconformity, timing, objectives, 'we' not 'me', imagination and drive. A common misconception is that to become a leader one must change one's personality. Leadership does not require becoming a different person; it merely requires a resourceful channelling of the special qualities that are buried inside you.

luck

Belief in luck, destiny, astrologers, and horoscopes is intrinsic to the Indian psyche. Everyone from the prime minister to the office peon believes in reading horoscopes. Yet few of us stop to analyse what we mean by luck – good or bad. The Webster dictionary defines luck as 'a force that brings good fortune or adversity'. Studies have revealed that luck is neither blind nor as chancey as we might think. There are growing indications that people who seemingly enjoy good luck in their careers and lives have a lot to do with 'directing' good fortune their way by the manner in which they conduct their conscious activities. Most successful people will agree that luck played an important role in their careers and they themselves had a great deal to do in steering Lady Luck in their direction (see Insight, Intuition, Good Timing, Kaleidoscopic Vision, Reasonable Risks and Warning Bells).

M

maintenance

Installing systems is all very well, but care must be taken that they are duly implemented and adequately maintained. The greatest danger for a successfully launched scheme is that two or three years down the line, sometimes maybe even less, people may lose initiative or the scheme itself might run out of steam. That's time to make sure you have checks and balances in place and adequate mechanisms to 'maintain' the efficiency of the system. Have refresher courses, review performances, appraise people periodically on identifiable performance standards, rotate staff, do whatever is needed to maintain that clear sense of purpose.

Remember, it isn't just machinery but manpower too that requires maintenance!

management by objectives (MBO)

An often-used word by management scientists such as Peter Drucker, MBO is a means of achieving goals. It should, ideally, be a process that involves as many people in the organisation as possible. For this, first the general objectives of the organisation must be outlined – the goals, purposes and direction it wishes to pursue. The general objective should then be pared down to specific targets, that is, 'We must increase sales by 15 per cent.' Each person who has drawn up a set of objectives must commit himself to the target. At the end of the specified time period, the manager must measure the levels of achievement. Suitable rewards based on achievement can be a part of the process (See Goals, Targets).

manager

Almost everyone wants to be a manager, if we go by the number of management schools mushrooming all over India or if we talk to any of the bright young men and women marching out with MBA degrees to conquer the world. The very word seems to carry so much prestige that it overshadows many other useful business functions. If you ask a young salesman why he wants to be a sales manager, his reply will be one of the following stock responses: It gives me status; I will become a decision-maker; It will expand my expense account; I will get a company car; or It will enhance my prestige within the company. These attitudes, though typical of many aspiring managers, reflect only one aspect of being a manager, namely, getting ahead. The role of a manager today is demanding, complex and varied. He has to be many things rolled into one. Primarily, he has to learn how to get results through people. To do so, he must know the skills, capabilities, experience and temperament of the people who work in his charge. He must be able to identify and select the right people and then integrate their individual talents into an effective team effort. A tall order, but then effective managers are quite used to that!

mediocrity

The mediocre are neither very good nor very bad; they are just average, ordinary (often very nice) people. In the words of one manager, 'They are not good enough to promote and not bad enough to fire.' They are the people who adjust, who alter their behaviour to fit and conform to the easy and the commonplace. They pull in their horns. They tune their receivers to the approved frequency. They are also the ones who are forever getting bypassed by younger, more efficient colleagues for promotions and perks.

Personal mediocrity is so prevalent (especially in public sector enterprises in India) that it is not only casually accepted but often stoutly defended. The most common attempt to rationalise mediocrity is the defence: 'Well, we need hewers of wood and drawers of water; you can't have all chiefs and no foot soldiers.' A closer look may reveal that a person who habitually adjusts to a mediocre level of performance is not necessarily of mediocre ability. Sometimes, usually unknowingly, the boss or the organisation fosters his 'adjustive-ness'. An effective manager must provide every employee with a choice between the passivity of adjustment and the activity of growth.

mistakes

Everyone makes mistakes – from the savviest business manager to the fumbling young sales rep. Reports of the latest bonehead move by someone in authority make newspaper headlines everyday. The worst thing about making a mistake is not learning from it. If you are a manager and you claim you have never made a mistake, you are not living up to your managerial responsibilities. People often make the error of viewing mistakes as failures. Their attitude is: 'Let's brush this under the carpet, fast.' Or they spend a lot of time and energy in finding someone to blame for the mistake. They obviously haven't learnt that mistakes can be opportunities to make improvements in the process that produced the error in the first place. A question like 'Why did you do this?' or a remark like 'How stupid can you get!' is going to put the person on the defensive. Ask the right questions to get to the root of the problem. Don't try to find a quick solution, tempting though it is to find a quick fix to limit the embarrassment flowing from the mistake. Finding out what really went wrong and involving everyone in the solution is a lot more effective.

money

Your earnings will rise as you move up the ladder of success and responsibility. So will your fringe benefits.

Moreover, you will also be able to change jobs more easily than before. Even the executive recruiters, better known as 'headhunters', will be coming after you. Have you ever taken note of the growing number of such agencies sprouting all over Delhi, Mumbai, Pune and other major cities? Their job is to be on the constant hunt for executive talent. Why? Because the chronic shortage of executive leaders is the greatest hunger of a burgeoning Indian economy galloping to catch up with its more evolved Asian counterparts in the race to capture market forces. Indeed, even government jobs, once considered the bastion of pen-pushers, are now attractively packaged to compete with the private sector. Even the leaders of free India have come to realise that patronage and nepotism are no substitute for corporate excellence. In such an environment attractive remuneration is the only real reward and recognition of success.

motivation

Like growth, motivation is inherent in every person. As a manager, your job is to press the right buttons and pull the right levers so that you are able to motivate your team to the right pitch to gain a common objective. Sometimes you take a soft approach, sometimes a hard tack, sometimes a combination of the two. Remember, different people require different tactics. It is often not easy to find a focus for dealing with motivation. Pitting competition with motivation can be a positive thing – especially in sales and marketing. Nothing motivates better than the feeling of going against someone who is bigger, better, stronger. Remember the strategy used by

Avis against the giant Levis: 'We are number two but we try harder.' As our economy was closed for many years, we lacked competition, and the perfectionists left us far behind many lesser-endowed nations. Post-liberalisation, post-reform 21st-century India needs all the motivation it can drum up to beat competitors such as China, Malaysia, Singapore, et al. About motivation, someone has rightly said:

It is so hard when I have to,
It is so easy when I want to.

N

network

Whether it is the old school-tie syndrome or the club factor, networks open many doors that would otherwise remain closed. In India we call this 'having the right connections' and being 'in the know'. There is no shortage of talented people in this world and there are many who never become successful because they have consistently kept their talents to themselves. Remember, if your circle of friends and acquaintances is large, your chances of being in the right place at the right time are considerably enhanced. A chance meeting or a chance word can lead to the right opportunity.

Make the largest number of contacts – business, social, and professional – that you can. The key to discovery is exposure. So cast your net far and wide.

new ideas

Most of the time one is not conscious of the need for new ideas even though one is grateful enough when they turn up! Sometimes one does not try and generate new ideas because one suspects that new ideas cannot be generated by trying. Most businesses require a continual flow of new ideas because you cannot go on flogging a dead horse. Even in the case of profit-making concepts and products, new ideas are essential. Many people suppose that new ideas mean new inventions or earth-shaking new discoveries. It need not always be so. Where is the need for inventing the wheel when the wheel already exists and is doing fine. New ideas include new ways of doing things, new ways of looking at things, new ways of organising things, new ways of presenting things, in fact, new ideas about ideas.

niche marketing

Even the biggies in today's business world want niches or special places under the sun. Niches have become so popular that even giants are now going after markets they once considered beneath their attention. Suddenly, small has become beautiful for the biggies. A market can be said to be divided into two segments. The first is the big slice dominated by a few large companies. Examples are cereals, soft drinks, computers, tyres, aluminium, and autos. In each of these industries, four to six giants divide 80-90 per cent of the market. Each company fights for an extra one per cent of the market which is worth hundreds of millions. The remaining small slice is comprised of hundreds of small concerns, each fighting for a nine per cent share of its one per cent specialised niche.

nonconformity

There was a time when a discreet tie and suit were mandatory for the successful corporate image. Not so now. Though the 'robots in gray flannel suits' have not completely disappeared from the boardrooms, men in jeans wearing Nike shoes and sporting long hair are also becoming visible – even in a country as conventional as India. Nonconformity, whether it is in dress or managerial style, is increasingly gaining acceptance. 'The style makes the man,' is an old adage. Individualists who can think for themselves can contribute more to the advancement, progress and uniqueness of any product or organisation. Remember the advertisement for Maggi Tomato Sauce: 'Boss, It's different!' But to what extent can you be "different"? There is no point in being a nonconformist just for the sake of being different from the mob. Exploit your best talents and traits and use them to show that you can make a unique contribution. That is the proper use of nonconformity.

office politics

Getting things done in organisations is often more complicated than it ought to be. Just having the best idea is not enough to ensure that it will be implemented, and having authority over others is rarely enough to guarantee that they will put forward their best efforts. Being a successful manager requires more than good ideas and latest management techniques. Effective managers go beyond the formal job descriptions and make things happen and get things done – despite all the pitfalls of petty politics that exist, in some degree or the other, in all offices. We Indians are a more politically conscious people than others, therefore we tend to be a more politically charged workforce. Politically savvy managers quickly learn how to get things done without getting done in themselves (See Open-Door Policy, Complainers, Employees, Performance Appraisal, Blame).

open-door policy

Many organisations speak proudly of their open-door policy, which they interpret to mean that any man in the organisation can walk into a manager's office and speak to him about any work-related subject. When the invitingly open door is accompanied by an open mind, it can be of great value to both the organisation and the individual. However, many managers apply the open-door policy in such a way that they inhibit rather than enhance the whole purpose of the exercise. Here are some questions you can ask yourself. Do you:

1. Welcome your subordinates, but keep the conversation minimal?
2. Make quick judgments and on-the-spot decisions instead of listening to the subordinates' problems and ideas?
3. Start leafing through your mail or place calls even while the man is talking?
4. Start cross-examining to find out how much or how little he knows?

If the answer is 'Yes' to any of the above questions, then you have missed the point of the open-door policy. You are there to listen, not talk; you have to show interest; you have to solve the problem; and above all, you have to make the man feel comfortable when he has summoned enough nerve to walk in through your door with his problem.

optimism

Optimists are positive people. They see the best in every situation. When they see a glass half filled with water, they say it is hall full; a pessimist would say it is half empty. Similarly, they see challenges rather than problems, likely benefits instead of risks, profits instead of losses. When someone puts forward a bright, innovative idea, the optimists zero in on the success rate rather than the possible failure.

P

paperwork

Some amount of paperwork is inevitable and an unnecessary evil – even in the most paperless office. Sometimes keeping it simple and basic is more useful than an over-sophisticated system. It is most likely to succeed if it is seen as a vehicle, not an end in itself.

people management

No amount of policies and procedures, fancy cafeterias, generous perks and fringe benefits, sparkling offices with lush green potted plants can take the place of managers who are genuinely interested in their people. The people who work for you and with you are your most valuable assets, so treat them wisely and treat them well. Your job as a manger is to get things done cost-effectively and efficiently through people. But people are not machines or brute animals. They have feelings and emotions and you can't get optimum work out of them, at least not in the long run, if you do not take into account their aspirations, hopes and wishes. If you treat them as you would want to be treated, if you have a real respect for them, if you recognise the fact that each one of them individually has a valuable contribution to make – then you are a good manager of people.

Those managers who deride such an approach as 'soft', usually do so because they do not understand people, or because they are afraid it will mean loss of power.

performance

What sort of businessman/manager/chief executive are you? For that matter, what sort of individual are you? Have you put your differential advantages of socio-economic background and education to any good use? Fortunately, in India we have a highly mobile society that allows us to make our own breaks and be where we want to be. Our progress can be measured by our record of accomplishments in school, college, in the jobs we have held and the position we enjoy in society.

Performance rather than potential is the acid test. The world is full of educated derelicts who once showed promise. Such men have lacked application and dedication to a task. As the Bible says, 'Show me a man who is diligent in his work. He shall stand before the kings'.

performance appraisal

Call them intangibles or extra contributions or whatever. Every manager in every business should have a means to pinpoint and evaluate employees' contributions that don't necessarily show up in black on the balance sheets at the end of each financial year. Your own personal system of appraisal could include: rewarding extra effort; recognising positive thinking and giving it the attention it deserves; letting employees take risks if your gut feeling tells you it is the sort of thing you yourself would have done; and above all, the best 'perk' you can give your subordinates is to show pride in their success. Sometimes all it takes to make a junior manager's day is when the Big Boss himself stops by at his office and says he has done a great job. One personal word of appreciation or recognition at the right time can be more important than the anonymous end-of-the-year performance appraisal reports.

periodic re-assessment

Periodic re-assessment means looking again at things that are taken for granted, things that seem beyond doubt; things that seem perfectly okay on the surface. Periodic re-assessment means challenging all assumptions. It is not a matter of re-assessing something because there is an urgent or pressing need to re-assess it; in fact, there may be no need at all for such an exercise. It is a matter of re-assessing something simply because it is there and has not been assessed for a long time. It is a deliberate and quite unjustified attempt to look at things in a new way. You may sometimes find that you have been wearing blinkers all along without realising. Periodic re-assessment gives you the opportunity to look afresh, take stock and make new decisions, if required (see Appraisal).

perseverance

The difference between perseverance and obstinacy is that one often comes from a strong will, and the other from a strong won't! A Chinese proverb says, 'If you get up one more time than you fall, you will make it through.' Most of the greatest inventions and discoveries in the world have been made possible by people who have kept on trying when there seemed to be no hope of success at all. Perseverance, then, is not about running one long race and winning it at all costs; it is many short races one after another. It is a race in which hanging on at all costs matters most, especially when others have let go.

personal power

What made Pandit Nehru and later his daughter, Indira Gandhi, stand out from the other leaders of their time? What made a Tata or an Ambani different from other wealthy industrialists? There is always a certain something that sets apart the truly great from the merely successful – in politics, in business, in every sphere of human enterprise. Personal power has nothing to do with how you look or how you dress; its most significant manifestation is how you deal with people. He who can convey understanding without having to spell it out laboriously and who can enlist cooperation and respect without having to invoke rank or the trappings of office has the most effective power over people. In its broadest sense, this means he has the ability to deal easily, comfortably and meaningfully with others. It also means he has the necessary insight both into his own self and into others. Such people have an underlying quality of personal warmth that is rooted in sincerity and expressed through openness. In the corporate world, such people always prove to be an invaluable asset.

personnel

Of all the various causes that can afflict your organisation, personnel problems are among the most common. Shortages of trained help, rapid shifts in requirements, and unforeseen problems take their toll. Added to this are the various labour-management tussles that can complicate the picture. How can you, as the manager, benefit from a personnel crisis? Simple. Analyse your personnel situation carefully and have answers ready for the boss when the crisis erupts. Everyone else will be running around wringing his hands. Not you! You will have some preparation and study under your belt. Be prepared to meet a crisis head-on and take full advantage of the situation for you can't wave a magic wand and make personnel problems disappear. You can only look into them sincerely and give them your best shot.

pirate-proofing

Capable professionals will always be in demand by outside recruiters and sometimes even be wooed by competitors.

A good manager can effectively retain his men who have potential and who would be more valuable on his side than the competitors'. The factors that make an individual vulnerable to outside offers are numerous, some lie in the individual, some in financial considerations, but most in the employee's immediate boss and the organisation itself. A manager contributes stability when he has a warm personal relationship with his subordinates. The understanding boss tends to hold his men by bonds of good communication and rapport that are necessary to solve their problems and make them feel valued and wanted. Providing enough challenges and allocating responsibility are still other ways of pirate-proofing your organisation. The wise executive delegates projects instead of segments of a job to an employee who is perfectly capable of working independently. The insightful manager recognises when an individual has become over-trained for his responsibilities and moves him on quickly to other things. A person held in a job beneath his abilities becomes increasingly resentful. This attitude makes him vulnerable to outside recruiters. Men of potential want to be associated with a company that provides opportunities for growth. A clear pattern of internal mobility, both vertically and laterally, is essential to hold people worth holding on to in their jobs.

positive attitude

Having a positive attitude means being:

- Non-judgmental;
- In control of one's self and situations;
- Creative in thinking and planning;

- Able to cope and effectively 'manage' change;
- Optimistic; and
- Able to effectively communicate all of the above attributes.

You don't have to be born with a positive attitude; you can certainly learn to be more positive about the things and people around you just as you can learn to be a more effective manager of people and situations. So, those who are not positive by nature can certainly become positive by nurture. Then, there can be certain factors in the work environment that can make you more positive, such as the salary you draw, your working conditions, behaviour of the management, variety and type of work you do, and the freedom of choice given to you by your superiors or other factors at play (see Optimism).

potential

No one knows what he or she can do till he or she tries it. Everyone has potential; all one needs to do is to make up one's mind as to what one wants to do and then stick to it. After that, there is no limit to where you can reach. Some people are late starters and reach their full potential quite late in life. Woodrow Wilson, US President, did not learn his letters till he was nine years old and couldn't read till he was eleven. Yet, he had the potential for greatness buried inside him; it took its own time to flower.

Those of us who play safe in life, never heed the possibility of what lies buried deep inside us, are people who have already decided that they don't want to grow anymore.

pragmatism

Some people condemn pragmatism because they believe that pragmatism seems to be a way of acting without principles. Pragmatism does not mean being unprincipled; it simply means the pragmatic use of principles. Pragmatism is when you do what can be done to achieve an objective and put as much emphasis on practicality as on principles. The main objection to pragmatism is that sometimes the end might come to justify the means. This can be avoided in business if your brand of pragmatism is concerned with where an action might lead – with the effect or consequences of the action – but it should not mean that anything is acceptable as long as you stand to gain. Pragmatism does not mean *chalta hai*. Ideally and strictly speaking, being pragmatic means being sensitive to a situation, to the people involved in the situation, and to what is practical.

preparation

Did you know, the Boy Scout motto is: Be Prepared. In life, as in chess, preparation is All! When you are prepared for something, the opportunity to use it, also presents itself. Take a good hard look at what appears to be someone's 'good luck'. You will find that behind the luck, there is actually a lot of preparation, planning and 'success-producing thinking'.

So, luck is actually little more than taking advantage of a situation at the right moment. It is possible to 'make' your luck act in your favour by being always prepared.

As Henry Kissinger had very wisely said, 'If we do what is necessary, all the odds are in our favour.'

For all your days prepare,
And meet them ever alike;
When you are the anvil, bear;
When you are the hammer, strike.

problem employees

Personality conflicts arise at home and at work for any number of reasons. At work managers refer to people they can't get along with as problem employees. Usually the problem that is causing the conflict or friction doesn't have anything to do with performance ability.

It may be tempting to let these people go, but that is taking the easy way out. Such people, no matter how troublesome they may be, must have useful skills. If they don't, why were they hired in the first place? Maybe you need to re-assess your hiring practices, if you end up with too many problem employees.

Sometimes a transfer can change the problematic behaviour. Sometimes, there can be a genuine grievance that is manifesting itself in aberrant behaviour. If you are able to 'salvage' a problem employee, you will send out a morale-boosting signal to the other employees and your stock as an effective manager will rise within the organisation. Remember, there aren't too many perfect employees, just as there aren't very many perfect managers. Being able to work with a problem employee is actually very good training for a good manager!

problem solving

You don't always have to go looking for problems; when problems are upon you, there is little choice but to try and solve them! A problem, simply defined, is the difference between what one has and what one wants. It may be a matter of avoiding something, of gaining something, of getting rid of something, or even of getting to know what one wants!

procrastination

Too many of us wait to do the perfect thing with the result we do nothing or wait forever for the right moment in order to do things perfectly. The way to get ahead is to start now. Like the Nike ad says: 'Just Do It.' Procrastination, or putting off for tomorrow, which can be done today, is letting the opportunity go by. Those who procrastinate say, 'I will seize the next opportunity that comes by' and let the present one pass. What they do not realise is that 'one of these days' is actually 'none of these days'.

R

reasonable risks

You do need to take risks in business. Nobody ever made it big by playing safe and sticking to the straight and narrow path. The secret is to make a distinction between reasonable risks and wild gambles.

Ask yourself two questions before making a rash decision: 'What is the worse thing that can happen if my decision is wrong?' and 'What is the best possible thing that can happen to me if my decision is right?' Remember, that the downside of risk-taking – failure – is only half the possible outcome.

The other possible outcome is success. Use this upside-downside formula for analysing and evaluating reasonable risk in all your major decisions. It will help you look at the possibility of both failure and success, and decide whether or not the risk is worth it.

responsibility

Gandhiji had said that every duty performed confers upon us certain rights, and the exercise of every right carries responsibilities and obligations. Responsibility for our actions is the one thing most people in positions of accountability hate, yet it is the one thing in the world that develops us the most and helps us reach our true potential.

Sometimes it becomes important to realise that we cannot escape the responsibility of tomorrow by evading it today. Remember always, freedom of thought, speech and action is a package deal – with it come responsibilities and consequences.

roadblocks to creativity

The following hindrances to creativity have to be guarded against:

1. Too much logic cramps or inhibits the imagination. Don't prejudice your ideas by saying they are 'too silly'.
2. Rigidity hampers the flow of creative ideas. Unless we 'let ourselves go' the flow of ideas will dwindle into a thin trickle. Try doing things a little differently, and you will find yourself becoming more flexible, hence more receptive to new ideas as they float in.

3. Timidity also slows down productive ideas. Many a good idea was lost because the originator of the idea was embarrassed or feared ridicule. The idea of the automobile and the aeroplane was ridiculed when it first appeared. Perseverance is the only antidote to timidity.
4. Self-discouragement may be fostered by a poor self-image or by failure to solve a problem, or both. Don't allow your imagination to be stifled by negative thoughts.

S

salesmanship

Selling is a way of life for all men of business at all levels within their organisations. Some companies have even evolved formal training programmes for employees because they believe that every employee is a salesman of his company's philosophy, personnel, service and products. The sales function is becoming increasingly critical, complex and yet one of the most misunderstood functions within an organisation. The popular stereotyped notion of a salesman in many people's mind is still that of a sophisticated, well-dressed, smooth-talking con man, an artist at deception and glib talk. Yet the salesman – that most misunderstood of all God's creatures – needs our sympathy and understanding rather than our scorn and derision. He has to be all things to all people – for him the customer is always right. He likes to talk not just because verbal skills are his chief asset, but also because it is through talking that he establishes an immediate rapport with the customer. He enjoys the psychological thrill that each sale brings him, but he also finds satisfaction in the service he has rendered to the customer and his own organisation. In the process, he has gained satisfied customers not victims. Good salesmanship, then, is a matter of positive persistence rather than abrasive intrusion and planned deception.

satisfaction

Satisfaction lies in treading a fine balance between too much satisfaction and too little. There is a proverb that says, 'I cried because I had no shoes until I saw a man who had no feet.' That is one aspect of satisfaction – the man who knows enough is enough will always have enough. But for some people merely enough is not enough; they want more. For such people the harder the struggle, the greater is the glory of achievement and triumph. Some people are never satisfied with what they have. In the final analysis, the amount of satisfaction you get from life depends on your own ingenuity, self-sufficiency and resourcefulness. People who wait around for life to supply them satisfaction usually find boredom instead.

scout

Plant your 'scouts' in the field who can bring you feedback about your product or business. Do some scouting yourself. Go to trade shows and exhibitions that relate to your business. There is no better way to stay on top of new developments. The expos and trade fairs organised by the Trade Fair Authority at Pragati Maidan in New Delhi are an instance where you can measure the opposition. Find out about other similar venues in your nearest city.

self-appraisal

Take a quick look at your own management style from time to time. Just how people-oriented is it? Does it contribute to, or detract from, efforts to build a stable organisation? What can you do to improve your management techniques and the results you are responsible for achieving? Ask yourself what you can do to build a strong foundation for future growth. Self-appraisal is very, very vital for any successful manager. Self-satisfaction or complacency is the first sign that the rot has set in. So you better watch out for those telltale signs of the slide downhill. Call yourself – and your organisation – to account. Is there anything you could have done differently, and for the better? Is there anything you have left undone, that you ought to have done (see Appraisal and Periodic Re-Assessment)?

self-deception

The first and worst of all frauds is the one who cheats himself. After that, all sin is easy. At the same time, this is one of the easiest sins. Nothing is so easy as to deceive one's self, for what we wish we readily believe. The sad part is that deception by friends, colleagues or others causes us immense hurt, yet self-deception seldom causes so much as a pang of regret.

self-respect

Self-respect is the cornerstone of all virtues. If you respect yourself, others will too. If you attach no value or respect to your own self, don't expect others to respect you for your talent, faculties and creative power. Insist on being your own self; never imitate.

Be true to yourself. Value yourself for what you are. When you start needing your self-worth to be approved of by others, or you start hankering after approval from others, it is tantamount to saying, 'Your view of me is more important than my own opinion of myself.' You are worthy of respect because you say it is so. If you depend on others to ratify your opinion of yourself, it becomes other-worth.

sorry

One simple word yet a whole book can be written on it – on its use and more often than not its lack of usage. A lot of misery, complications and trouble can be avoided if people only learn to say 'Sorry' at the right time. When a company or individual realises he has made a mistake, there is no sense in compounding that mistake with another mistake: hanging on stubbornly because of ego. It is far better to give in gracefully and admit your mistake, soothe ruffled feathers and make a mental note to avoid making the same mistake again!

stress

Stress can do untold damage to you. It can even be a killer if allowed to continue unchecked. First find out what is causing it, then set about relieving it. Job-related stress is caused by both internal and external factors. The external causes are easier to identify. These can be exorbitant workload, mountains of paperwork, unrealistically tight schedules and perennial time pressures. If the job itself is causing stress or any of the following is placing you in a stressful situation – role ambiguity; sense of under-achievement; insecurity and feeling of being threatened – then your problems are internal. For that you need to do some good hard thinking and seek professional help.

stress management

Once you have pinpointed the reasons that are causing you stress, the next logical thing is to find way(s) to handle it. There are as many ways to handle stress as there are causes. Here's a collection of stress-relieving techniques that are known to work. Pick out ones that might work for you. You can come up with your own permutations and combinations: exercise; take a hot bath or soothing drink; talk of your innermost fears with someone you know and trust; give yourself a little 'treat' if you have handled something to your satisfaction; don't look back and worry over spilt milk; make a decision instead of dithering, procrastination is a leading cause of heartburn; stop to smell the roses once in a while, take a break to enjoy life's small pleasures; put some variety into your life; change rigid patterns to include newer experiences; keep an open mind, for resistance to change has caused many good managers to lose sleep; and like the song says: 'Don't worry, be happy!'

study

Check out magazines, trade journals, newspapers, anything you can lay your hands on to find out about new developments in your field or new technologies that could influence your product or area or specialisation, whatever that might be. Pay particular attention to news about competitors, competitive products or services. Don't stop there. Look around you. Study human nature. Look outside your particular field for new ideas or innovative concepts you could apply to your business.

success

If you want success in life make perseverance your best friend. Remember, eighty per cent of success is sheer hard work and dogged perseverance. The remaining twenty per cent is contributed by attention to small details, preparation and opportunity. No one becomes successful by luck alone. Success in business is the sum of small efforts, repeated day in and day out. But before you score, you must have a goal. So identify a target you want to achieve. No one ever drifted towards success.

The first and most important step towards success is the feeling that, yes, I will succeed. Success is a state of mind. If you want success, start thinking of yourself as a success.

Make your mistakes stepping-stones and learning experiences. Leave nothing to chance. Take courage from the fact that the season of failure is the best time to sow the seeds of success.

supervisor

A supervisor is part of the managerial team. He controls the activities of others and has the responsibility of carrying out the management's policies and intentions by leading the group under his charge. To members of the team, he is the immediately visible 'face' of the management. Not only must a supervisor know his own job thoroughly, he must also know the management structure above him as well the team under him. A supervisor's role is more than 'keeping an eye' on the team allotted to him or keeping his ears open to report to the bosses.

He is the crucial link between top management and the lower rungs. He is the person most likely to spot any lowering of standards at the earliest. He is the most effective fire-fighter-cum-classroom monitor. Sometimes he can dispense immediate justice and address grievances, even deal with personal matters that need not land at the manager's already cluttered table.

T

talking

As someone very wisely said, they talk most who have least to say. Wise men talk because they have something to say; fools because they would like to say something. It is a sad thing when men have neither the wit to speak well, nor judgment to hold their tongues. Words are your most precious commodity, so spend them judiciously.

You don't have to launch into mindless chatter to fill silences. Be careful never to talk of personal matters – neither your own nor other people's – at work. Learn how to listen and you will profit even from those who talk badly. Your manner of talking is a reflection of your personality. Do you talk clearly, coherently and crisply? Do you mean what you say? Do you listen to others as well as you talk? Do you talk in order to communicate effectively or merely to hear your own voice? For good or bad, your manner of talking is like an advertisement. Every time you open your mouth you let others look into your mind. Do they see it well clothed, neat and business-like? The choice is yours.

target

As a general rule targets should be placed at a level that is challenging but attainable. Practically speaking, there is little point in setting unrealistic targets since it can sometimes be counter-productive and lead to low self-esteem among the employees. A good manager will, where possible, discuss the advisability and appropriateness of any target with the rest of his team.

Another thing with targets is, they can't be rushed in the last lap always; the thing to do is to set off on the right foot by making the correct beginning and setting the right pace. In business, as in life, the first thing you must do is to decide what you really want. What is the target you are working towards? Weigh the costs and the results.

Are the results worthy of the costs? Then make up your mind and go for the target with all your might – full steam ahead! There is a flip side to targets; the greatest danger often is not that our target is too high or too unattainable and we might miss it, but that it is too low and we reach it too easily. If that is the case, you are undermining your own self and capabilities (see Management by Objectives).

teamwork

Teamwork is like happiness; the more pointedly we go after it, the more it eludes us. And like happiness, teamwork is a byproduct, a natural corollary, an almost spiritual feeling that accompanies joint activities. Most people like to feel they are part of a team because it makes them feel more secure. If the team approach to work is stressed, each employee is going to feel that it is important for him or her to make a contribution, which will make your job as the manager all the more easier.

The idea is to let it be known that your team is more important than any single individual, no matter how worthy he or she may be. Here is what you can do to enhance the team spirit in your organisation or department: Be frank and open while communicating; Discuss complaints/problems openly and objectively; Keep personal issues confidential within the team; Never blame each other when things begin to go wrong; Don't put personal interests before team interests; and Share resources/information equally with all team members.

test marketing

Business surveys, unlike the polling done for political candidates, are aimed more at preventing failure than assuring success. In today's unpredictable business environment, it is hard to tell whether even the best of products and services will sell. A CEO may come up with an ingenious idea that the board of directors might buy, but the public might not accept the same. Even proven ideas sometimes need to be re-evaluated and re-vamped – a bit like putting old wine in new bottles or vice versa. There are no constants in business because people keep changing. Test marketing can check the viability of a new product and also gauge the public's reaction to an old product that has been given a facelift.

thinking and thought

One thought at a time. Just like a computer can handle only one operation at a time, so the human mind handles only one thought at a time. It is important to understand and accept this reality and to monitor your thoughts. There are many different kinds of thoughts: constructive, inventive, creative, optimistic, stimulating, and many other positive thoughts. There are also negative thoughts, such as: destructive, pessimistic, depressing. One needs to be aware that positive thoughts lead to positive results and negative thoughts lead to destruction and misery. All life is essentially a game of thought; you can make up the rules as you go along. You can, to a large extent, decide your thoughts. You can keep negative thoughts at bay and focus on the positive ones. You can even train yourself to dwell more on the positive side of things.

time

Money can be replaced but time lost is gone forever. It is a non-renewable resource. The first and most important step in improving your time utilisation is planning; it helps cut down on time wastage drastically and gives focus to your actions. Ask yourself:

- What, precisely, do you want to get done?
- In what order of importance?
- Over what period of time?
- What is the time available?
- What is the best strategy for application of time to projects for the most effective results?

tradition

Just because things have always been done in a certain way is no reason why they should continue to be done in exactly the same way forever. A healthy respect for tradition is one thing, but a blind adherence to the past is quite another. The antiquity and general acceptance of an opinion, view or practice is not an absolute assurance of its truth. Revere the traditions and time-honoured practices by all means, especially if yours is a family-owned enterprise, but do not hold on to the old at the cost of the new. To follow imperfect, uncertain or corrupted or distorted traditions simply in order to avoid making an error of judgement or because you lack the confidence to introduce changes, is but to exchange one danger for another.

troubles

Troubles are often the tools by which God fashions us for better things. They don't harm us in any long-term way – unless we break down under them and turn bitter and sour, narrow and cynical. There is little purpose served in dwelling upon one's troubles; it is far better to treat troubles as learning experiences and to put them behind. The wise manager can even find a blessing in the troubles that rain down on him. He can treat them as brooms and shovels that smooth the road to better fortune.

trust

You can't do business with someone you don't trust. It is as simple as that. But trust is a two-way street. You have to trust others in order to be trusted by them. Above all, you have to trust yourself and your own innermost feelings. Unfortunately, a lot of people do not trust themselves and the judgements and decisions they make. This leads to confusion and disharmony all around. A few betrayals do not mean that you stop trusting your fellow workers.

type a and type b personalities

These are terms from psychology that have passed into common usage. The world of business and commerce, like any other profession, has its share of both types. Type A's are aggressive, dedicated to achieving more in the least possible time, extremely competitive, and most likely to set unrealistic targets and deadlines. They are more driven, more 'hyper' in many ways and more achievement-oriented in terms of monetary or other rewards. Though outwardly confident, even brash, they often have a deep-rooted sense of insecurity. They are also more likely to develop heart disease at an early age and suffer from peptic ulcers and hypertension. The guy in the car behind you frantically blowing his horn because you were a fraction of a second late when the traffic light turned green, or the one who jostles you by the kerbside as he whizzes past to catch the light before it turns red – is in all likelihood a Type A personality.

Type B's are just the opposite. They are more laid-back, less aggressively cut-and-thrust and less demanding – though by no means less effective in their work. They too will get the job done, but in a far more low-key and less flamboyant manner than the Type A's.

U

unhappiness

Unhappiness is not knowing what we want and killing ourselves to get it. It lies in not knowing what our goals are, where we are heading and where we want to be in the future and complaining that we are drifting aimlessly and not doing anything worthwhile while others are charging ahead. Unhappiness is not a personal matter alone; it affects others in the team and organisation, therefore it needs to be given importance even in a work-related context. One person's unhappiness can sometimes be contagious and can influence the atmosphere of the whole office.

Many people think if they were only in some other place, or had some other job, they would be happy. That is doubtful since happiness, and unhappiness, are both a state of the mind. And, both are temporary. Just as the good things don't last, unhappiness too is temporary. When the going gets tough, tell yourself: This too shall pass.

unpredictability

Alas, things are not what they used to be! This is a common refrain, especially among the older executives. But there is little to be gained by bemoaning a fast-changing world that keeps throwing up new challenges. The business environment is no longer what it used to be even till a generation ago. Crystal ball gazing is futile in this volatile and unpredictable scenario. Traditionally, CEOs want concrete figures and watertight predictions from their managers: 'Give me a number.' In an era of unpredictability, this doesn't make sense. A forecast is binding; you are committed to it; your reputation is at stake. So, don't make forecasts; make assumptions instead. There's a big psychological difference. You can adjust your assumption without losing face. Remember: More knowledge means more unpredictability, not less. Along the information highway and through the internet, we have entered a new age – the age of knowledge. The increase in knowledge has created better educated, more sophisticated consumers – another reason for increased unpredictability.

V

values

Everyone values things differently. In other words, they place their own value on things that affect their lives according to their own value systems and perceptions. Though intangible assets and values are the core of our soul, and by extension, our businesses too.

They are those beliefs – inherited or acquired and accumulated over a period of time – that make one individual distinct from others. Most of our behaviour can be traced to our beliefs and thereby to our values.

Going against our values can produce deep conflicts and result in much unhappiness and dissatisfaction with our self and eventually the work that we do. Analyse and know your own value system – what works best for you and what goes against the grain. At the same time, become sensitive to the values that others prize and cherish. Above all else, never waiver from your own deeply rooted values. A little profit is a small thing to lose compared to losing your sense of values.

W

warning bells

Wishful thinking is not intuition. Neither should hope be confused with hunch. As psychologists warn, 'Failure to maintain some degree of pessimism is to be in a state of peril.' So don't disregard those nagging voices trying to tell you what you don't want to hear. All of us have a natural tendency to hear the voice of intuition only when it tells us something good is going to happen. As a good manager you have to learn to heed the warning bells also when they begin to set off an alarm inside you. They may come bearing a career-saving message. No one is immune to failure, or let us say a cross-connection between a warning bell and an intuitive flash. The thing to do is to let your native skepticism take over. Instead of shooting from the hip, let cool judgment decide the issue. At the same time, give the warning bells the attention they deserve. They are valuable in-built tools, placed inside your body by a combination of nature, experience and training (see Hunch and Intuition).

wealth

The way to wealth is as plain as the way to market. It depends chiefly on two things: industry and frugality, that is, waste neither time nor money, but make the best use of both. Without industry and frugality nothing will do; and with them, everything. It requires a great deal of boldness and a great deal of caution to create wealth, and when you have made it, it requires ten times as much intelligence to keep it. In that sense, inherited wealth can be a great handicap to ambition. It is good to have things that money can buy, but it is also good to check up once in a while and be sure one has things money can't buy!

wide-angle vision

It has been said that a man with a hammer will only see nails. So also the man who suffers from tunnel vision will only see that which is straight ahead. The truly creative manager will look at the world around him through a wide-angle lens taking in the view in one grand panoramic sweep. He can pick up vital clues for his business in seemingly unrelated fields.

Wide-angle vision also includes peripheral vision – something most good athletes also possess. It is the ability to look at everything, focusing on nothing, until the last moment of commitment when you zero in on the object faster than the eye can blink. All good businessmen unconsciously exercise wide-angle vision, spotting new opportunities all over the place, while their less-gifted counterparts merely concentrate on raking up profits by focusing narrowly on the bottom line. Those naturally gifted with wide-angle have an uncanny ability to see and play the game several moves ahead of their opponents. This need not be a God-given gift; it can be cultivated by getting out of the *kuain ka mendhak* (frog-in-the-well) attitude and taking in everything that is happening around you.

winning

Vince Lombardi had once said: 'Winning is not everything; but making the effort to win is.' An employee who gives his or her best is a winner regardless of who eventually bags the big contract. Being able to adjust is a necessary attribute of winning in today's business world. Some managers and organisations thrive on change, while others throw up their hands in despair, without even putting up a good fight and sink into oblivion. Self-confidence is the other vital prop of the psychology of winning. If you can instill confidence in your employees, they may yet give you their best – even when they are in a losing position.

worry

Do you remember things that you worried and fretted over a year ago? Do you remember how they worked out? Did you or did you not waste a lot of time and fruitless energy over them? Didn't most of them turn out all right after all? In fact, a year later you would be hard pressed to answer why you worried over those things at all. Worry kills more people than work. There are some people who can dodge an elephant but not a fly. Worry is today's mice nibbling on tomorrow's cheese.

Z

zero-error margin

Scale by itself is no longer sufficient in a world where margins are tight and competition comes from so many quarters. An excellent product is a good thing in itself but when combined with scale you can create a very powerful, sustainable, competitive advantage. At every stage of a product manufacture, you need to build in checks and balances that will reduce and finally eliminate the possibility of error. When there is absolutely no room for error in a race, when you have reduced the possibilities of things going wrong not just to the bare minimum but have eliminated the possibility of making an error, you can safely say you have achieved the zero-error margin. It refers to that 'edge' or 'point' beyond the minimum necessary, going the extra mile in executing an activity, analysing records of present and past operations, studying trends and estimates and forecasting a stage which is devoid of human error.

zipf's law

According to G.K. Zipf, human behaviour is governed by the Principle of Least Effort. Human beings, at home or at work, display a natural tendency to put in the minimum amount of effort to achieve a certain goal.

All of us are guilty of this: whether consciously (as in taking a shortcut) or unconsciously (as when we forget to cross our t's and dot our i's). The more ardent followers of Zipf's Law fall under the category of shirkers.

They are the ones who can cause most damage to an organisation. A good manager must keep a sharp eye out for such shirkers and gradually wean them out of positions of responsibility.

"The only time-tested formula you can bring to your personal management equation is – Experience. Perhaps, one day you too can compile your own handbook of management – an A-Z of management based on your own uniquely personal experiences – to hand over to those who follow in your footsteps, your protégés, heirs, sons and daughters."

Rakhshanda Jalil